REGISTERS OF ILLUMINATED VILLAGES

Also by Tarfia Faizullah

Seam

REGISTERS

OF

ILLUMINATED

VILLAGES

POEMS

TARFIA FAIZULLAH

Graywolf Press

This publication is made possible, in part, by the voters of Minnesota through a Minnesota State Arts Board Operating Support grant, thanks to a legislative appropriation from the arts and cultural heritage fund, and a grant from the Wells Fargo Foundation. Significant support has also been provided by Target, the McKnight Foundation, the Lannan Foundation, the Amazon Literary Partnership, and other generous contributions from foundations, corporations, and individuals. To these organizations and individuals we offer our heartfelt thanks.

Published by Graywolf Press
250 Third Avenue North, Suite 600
Minneapolis, Minnesota 55401

www.graywolfpress.org

Published in the United States of America

ISBN 978-1-55597-800-6

2 4 6 8 9 7 5 3

Library of Congress Control Number: 2017938024

Cover design: Mary Austin Speaker

Cover art: Shahzia Sikander, *Pleasure Pillars*, 2001. Watercolor, dry pigment, vegetable color, tea and ink on hand-prepared wasli paper. © The artist, courtesy of Sean Kelly, New York.

for y'all
shobar jonno

CONTENTS

←

REGISTERS OF ILLUMINATED VILLAGES

I do not count the time.
Nina Simone

REGISTER OF ELIMINATED VILLAGES

> I have a register which lists 397 eliminated villages, Kurdish villages in
> northern Iraq. . . . The work is called "The Register of Eliminated Villages."
> It's a very decorative, pretty thing . . .   —Kanan Makiya, *Frontline*

Somewhere in this insomniac night
       my life is beginning
without me. In Northern Iraq,
       it is high noon, the sun there

perched over fields shriven
       with lilies, the petals of orange
poppies red with a light
       that a gauze of gray sparrows

glides through over sheaves
       of bone too stubborn to burn,
all that is left of those razed
       towns. A mother turns to a father

in the cold room they share,
       offers her hands to his spine.
I curl inside her, a silver bangle
       illuminated by candle's

flame. I curl beside you, lay
       my head close to the vellum
of your smooth back and try
       again to sleep. Count to one

thousand, you suggest. Count to two.
       Three. As someone must count
hacked date trees, hollowed
       hills paved into gardens, though

the scholar on tonight's
               Frontline only counted each
town destroyed: three
               hundred ninety-seven of them.

Who counts dolls, hand-
               stitched, facedown in dirt?
Count to four. Five. Six. Count
               cadaver, stone, belongings: pots,

spun from red clay. Who
               will count the amputated
hands of thieves? A mother
               presses a hand to me. Inside

her, I thrash, a stalk of wheat
               blistered by storm. Sleep comes,
brief as it is bright. I startle
               awake, turn to you. The register,

I know, is real,
               fat with the names of the dead,
elegant strokes of sharp pencil
               etched into thick pages. A father

presses an ear to a mother's
               belly. I am wide awake. Count
to seven. Eight. Nine. You
               murmur, turn to me. Someone

must be counting hours
               spent weaving lace the color
of moonlight for a girl's
               dowry. But I don't have

the right to count hours,
                    girls, dowries—just the skin-
thin pages of the good book
                    I once cut a hollow into,

condoms I stored there,
                    cigarettes. Count each minute
I waited for them to fall
                    asleep. Count nights I sat alone

on the curb, held smoke
                    inside my mouth, released
whorls of it into the air.
                    A father leaves a mother asleep

on her side, the crocus
                    of my fetus nestled inside.
I draw over us the thin
                    sheet. A father reaches

for the Qur'an, thumbs through
                    page after illuminated page,
runs his finger beneath
                    each line of verse, looks everywhere

for the promise of my name.

THE HIDDEN REGISTER OF HUNGER

(Selfish)

to touch the swan-soft aperture
between a sleeping baby's
shoulder blades,

(common)

like dirt-new graves, like the seams
of stockings we skim
our hands down the length of,

searching for the memory
of the first ancient feeling
we ever had. It's easy

(hollow)

to laugh in bed with a new lover
at the same joke, and know
energy always precedes

matter, but here's craving anyway
in my begging body, fat
with powdered milk.

Why angel before serpent,
why plucked rib before desire?
Here, I hold both ends

of my spine. There, pickled mango spoons

(greed)

into a clay bowl for our pleasure. O, these daily
rituals we believe we are owed.
O, arrogant, tongue-slung,

costume-replete closets
of our lives in which we assume

(time)

will still be there, a bare lightbulb
burning. Memory pours starfish into the sky
for us to imagine, and still

we burn. O, tendons of our unbearable
master plans. O, maa, maa, maa.
If we're going to use knives,

then we should learn how to carve

(flesh)

by whittling our false gods from stone.

SELF-PORTRAIT AS MANGO

She says, *Your English is great! How long have you been in our country?*
I say, *Suck on a mango, bitch, since that's all you think I eat anyway.* Mangoes

are what margins like me know everything about, right? Doesn't
a mango just win spelling bees and kiss white boys? Isn't a mango

a placeholder in a poem folded with burkas? But this one,
the one I'm going to slice and serve down her throat, is a mango

that remembers jungles jagged with insects, the river's darker thirst.
This mango was cut down by a scythe that beheads soldiers, mango

that taunts and suns itself into a hard-palmed fist only a few months
per year, fattens while blood stains green ponds. Why use a mango

to beat her perplexed? Why not a coconut? Because this "exotic" fruit
won't be cracked open to reveal whiteness to you. This mango

isn't alien just because of its gold-green bloodline. I know
I'm worth waiting for. I want to be kneaded for ripeness. Mango:

my own sunset-skinned heart waiting to be held and peeled, mango
I suck open with teeth. *Tappai!* This is the only way to eat a mango.

ACOLYTE

The white cross pales
further still,
     nailed arms
watchful as window-light

furls over the backs
of our knees,
     as lavender shadows
cut off our little

necks. I am an infidel
in this classroom
     church. I kneel with
the other, restless

on the cracked leather
kneeler. I crave these
     pillars of candle.
My mouth is avid; it

sings *fidelis, fidelis.*
My maa is in her
     kitchen crooning
black-and-white film

songs that curl her
hennaed fingers
     around the rolling pin's
heavy back and forth.

My baba leans forward
in his chair, the Qur'an
          open to the last
page, the dark words

blurring as his eyes close
to reconcile again the shapla-
          shaped epitaph
on his father's tombstone.

With my head bowed,
I whisper, "Amar naam
          Tarfia," until it is
a prayer that grows.

I help stack the hymnals
higher; I cup the candle
          away. I cry out, "Bismillah!"
before I disrobe.

YOUR OWN COUNTRY

. . . that wasn't the same day two towers staggered into the ground. You were warned they'd be hunting us. But you didn't want to be soft. There's a first day you learn a country can't be earned. Your heart's embarrassed eesh-oof. It is soft. It isn't soft at all. A shiny pickup drives past. *Go back to your own country!* they holler. A firecracker, lit then thrown. There's a first day you learn *ours* and *theirs.* The girl with curious fingers says hello. Her friend's scorn. *You'll get whatever they have!* The skylight pours down all that white at home. *What about the poor people in our country? Do you want to be like them? Is that it? Then go. Go.* There's a first day you learn how to kill yourself without dying. Your own country demands it. It isn't new. It isn't news.

THE SACRIFICE

—Qurbani Eid

No, I said. *I want
to watch them behead
the goat*
                    with the men.
Her eyes glistened
as the scythe sang
down
                    her neck
and spine. *I'm proud
of you,* the uncles said. *It is
important*
                    to observe
death. Her hoof, cleaved
from her shin. Her belly.
Everywhere
                    I looked
was trickling ant-shadow.
Pleasant banter. Her blood.
The aunts
                    came out
to slide the chopped acres
of her into hissing oil
and onion.
                    She was
steam-soft and spice-bold.
I ate her between my cousins,
licked
                    my palm across
the blood-gravy of what was left
on the filigreed china. Yes,
I savored

her more than
once: first with rice, then with
chutney. My first death. I felt
curious,
                    conflicted. Satisfied.

IV AND MAKE-UP HOMEWORK

How was your summer vacation?

There was an accident, then shoulder bone
                    shatter. There was an accident
and then an operation
           and then another operation
                        and then another knifing after.

What's one thing you learned this summer?

The only way to test
                for nerve damage is to pierce
each one with a needle; in
                        and out of my limp arm, the thread-thin
      stainless steel purls. Across me, so many
                    small holes.

What are your plans today?

Mornings begin anyway.
        Another vein in my left hand opens for the IV.
        My hand is a snail-curled
                fist; no one look!
                                To atrophy.

List at least three books you read this summer.

I pry open the closet door at night with *A Wrinkle in Time* and a penlight.
Zev, Abraham, and Isaac.
I pry open phonebooks and recite the names of strangers.
I pry one finger from my fist to drag under lines of black-finned Arabic.
The doctor pries open with latex gloves the dank wound.

The doctor packs gauze into the dark wound.
My medical record.

What's your favorite color?

Dark smudge. Unerasable, left on homework I wake each morning to finish at
the old dining-room table.

Look up the definition of a word you learned this summer.

infection (n): corrupted, corroded, or adulterated condition, an adulterating
substance, an impurity, moral contamination; corruption of character or habits
by evil influences; an instance of this, communication of bad or harmful beliefs
or opinions; an instance of this, the communication of a feeling or quality from
one person to another through example or contact; an instance of this; disease;
an epidemic, the condition produced by this; the corruption of faith; an instance
of this, an instance of this, this instance, this   *this*

Describe your current situation.

Attached to me, this new limb:
        the bag of antibiotics on its metal stand
near to bursting. My needle-pierced
                                        hand, the tape too tight,
corrupt and unclean, morbid: words
                                in a file with my name.
You will want to remember this suffering later.
        A picture.

What else did you learn this summer?

I learned to write my name with both hands,
        to pile rice into a fort with a fork;
I learned matter and energy are the same thing,
        to look away when the shutter clicks closed.

WEST TEXAS NOCTURNE

Because the sky burned, I had to unhinge
from the window the mesh screen
to step out onto the roof where the world was
an orange freshly peeled. I held

to my nose fingertips scented with spring.
Beside me fluttered the wings
of another promise I made but didn't keep.
I sat there for hours until my thighs

were raw, ripped by those rough shingles.
I knew how to perform under the gun,
to tether myself farther and farther afield.
This was before the other daughter

died and only one of us cried, but long after
those old pumpjacks no longer
needled the horizon clean. The velvet mat stayed
unfolded, but I told y'all I prayed

anyway. The sky was famished with stars.
I couldn't help but count each scorched one.

THE PERFORMANCE OF NO ONE'S FINGERS

Before your final recital, I threw
        my own shit at Maestro,
which is all I knew of love
        until you showed up: cleaner,
I'm told, than my own struggle,
        a keening mouth refusing
or unwilling to take hold.

Maestro would make me practice
        spelling (*abnegation, aborigine,*
artifact) while you slept soundly,
        violin beside you on its own pillow.
I envied you enough to pretend
        to have fallen asleep, and even
arranged the spelling primer

into a winged weight across my chest.
        Still, Maestro shook me awake
to mouth into the cicada-slick hours
        a bunch of words whose meanings
I didn't have to know to spell correctly.
        "Abar, abar!" Maestro urges
in beetle-blistered memory . . .

So many performances later, I forget
        you nightly. There's so much I didn't
say, or maybe I just need to hold
        your hand again through another
too-long interlude. I still feign sleep
        on nights I can't bear the legato
of anyone's fingers across me,

though *artifact* no longer eludes
        me. Sister, aborigine memory,
I stood beside your grave, but did not
        cry. I abnegated what we used to be,
and tried to be prodigy enough
        for four. Still, there are nights I can't
sleep and hear only your elegant détaché—

no one can keep you away—
        you lift the bow to the strings
of the violin I'd do anything
        to see you play, pray, play.

DJINN IN NEED OF A BITCH

The overpass's graffitied asphalt
drapes heavy shadows over pickup
trucks coasting always elsewhere,

while the humid city continues
to glisten with bodies, their crevices
hidden by cotton or lace, fingernails

bitten to the quick before scraped
down a sweat-brocaded torso, knees
shawled by soft or calloused palms.

Forget the sounds of glass shattering,
the alleyways I walk past, hunger
a thin blade knifing me cleaner.

Forget the shaking and raving man
I still see, for years now. Forget his voice
burning past me. *Bitch, I need you,*

bitch, I need, I need, he moans,
and I know it's not me he wants, but
the night is a varnished peeling wall

against which I, too, want again to be
roughly pressed. How many other nights
has he stumbled across this heat-neoned

sidewalk, pleaded with someone else
who isn't there? Low-riders bend corners
with earthquakes of bass, crackle of voices

strafe the air thirsty: thigh, throat, clavicle,
crook of elbow, curve of breast. *Bitch, I need,
I need*, and I never know if I want

to remember or forget those summers
spent sleeping underground in that old
peach-carpeted basement, how my sister

was once safe and warm beside me
the night I heard footsteps that weren't
any of ours. I took her smaller hand

in mine, waited until dawn
when the footsteps finally ceased: dream-
summoned, alive, or ghostly, I'll never know.

But what does that have to do with writhing
hips, tug of earlobe, the shock of new lips? *I need,
I need*, and the craving inside of me isn't

for food, and I can't ignore feeling
I've never belonged anywhere:
not this city or that village,

not in childhood's cradle, not this adult bed
I slide into alone after crying out
your name, O, Allah. Tell me why being

your disciple is so lonely, why this man
turns to no one beside him, tries
to embrace her. Tell me why the dead

are mirages stepping lightly across
the floors of strangers, their children
asleep below. Allah re, tell me why

you made it so that taking a kiss
full on the mouth feels like weeping:
the helpless swell, its delicious

spill. *I need. I need.*
Take then, as you took her too.

FEAST OR FAMINE

When the night gapes wider,
the child you once were
wakes and chokes with hunger
and you begin to soothe her

as you always do: first with hunger
and then more hunger,
because it's summer,
because the days are longer,

because you have to keep her lean,
because yes, she has to learn
to want, because yes, she has to train
to run through spring,

its melting forests,
to follow the path of pines,
far from her parents,
far from anyone who pins

her to herself after stubbing out lit
cigarette after lit cigarette
on her thighs. When the night
bloats open, tell the little

girl you still are and once were
to go back to sleep, go curl
inside the rise-and-fall of the warmth
asleep beside you—the one who loves her

and you—that she doesn't have to deny
the past anymore, that in Bangla, "kheeda
laage" can mean *I feel hunger*
and *I want you*, that the swell of the belly

only disappears when she starves
too. "Kheeda laage," you say to the one who strokes
her hair and devours
your mouth, and the destroyers

whittle into whispers flayed of their lost
appetites—listen.

BEFORE THE ACCIDENT, AND AFTER

I promise to lose weight was a lie
I told in every register I knew, until
the night the wind blew backward,
and exactly seven yellow poppies grew
from the mouth of her corpse I tried
to cuddle. I then began to count
the number of times my insomniac
friend said the word *tomorrow*,
the number of years any cactus
outlasted my sister, pound after pound
of the weight I lost then gained—
            my gravy-thick horror.
My piles of chicken-bone sorrow.
I tried to stop missing my little sister
so I could better love my pretty mother,
shadows engraved in the secrets
of her wedding bangles. But no one wanted
to kiss me, and it doesn't matter. *Fat*
is a silver vessel that holds holy water.
I was fat before the accident, and fat after.

100 BELLS

My sister died. He raped me. They beat me. I fell
to the floor. I didn't. I knew children,
their smallness. Her corpse. My fingernails.
The softness of my belly, how it could
double over. It was puckered, like children,
ugly when we cry. My sister died
and was revived. Her brain burst
into blood. Father was driving. He fell
asleep. They beat me. I didn't flinch. I did.
It was the only dance I knew.
It was the kathak. My ankles sang
with 100 bells. The stranger
raped me on the fitted sheet.
I didn't scream. I did not know
better. I knew better. I did not
live. My father said, I will go to jail
tonight because I will kill you. I said,
She died. It was the kathakali. Only men
were allowed to dance it. I threw
a chair at my mother. I ran from her.
The kitchen. The flyswatter was
a whip. The flyswatter was a flyswatter.
I was thrown into a fire ant bed. I wanted to be
a man. It was summer in Texas and dry.
I burned. It was a snake dance.
He said, Now I've seen a Muslim girl
naked. I held him to my chest. I held her
because I didn't know it would be
the last time. I threw no
punches. I threw a glass box into a wall.
Somebody is always singing. Songs
were not allowed. Mother said,

Dance and the bells will sing with you.
I slithered. Glass beneath my feet. I
locked the door. I did not die. I did
not die. I shaved my head. Until the horns
I knew were there were visible.
Until the doorknob went silent.

THE HIDDEN REGISTER OF SUBMISSION

The girl loosens

(shame)

the purple ribbon
from her hair and flings it
into a corner.

She can't bear that no one
touches her and learns
to plumb

(ego)

herself. She flowers between
in-betweens: shadows
she picks her way out of,

struggling between doorway
and hallway,
between clit and kiss

(devotion)

too hungry to stay put.
*You should never have
agreed to be a god*

*for me if you were afraid
to assume
the duties of a god . . .*

(absolution)

she smokes,
grinds out her stubs
under the well-scuffed sole
of a high-heeled boot.

Submit, on all fours
press your forehead low,

(absolution)

cover yourself, uncover
yourself, cover thighs,
throat, clover calves, honeysuckled
arm-bones, uncover

hips unmarked by anyone's
protests or plans, cover up, cover

up, up, down, now down, yes, down, uncover
clefts of unkissed collarbones, polish
up those cuffs, show off your worth, now tie

(absolution)

the purple ribbon in your hair extra tight.

SELF-PORTRAIT AS SLINKY

It's true I wanted
    to be beautiful before
        authentic. Say the word
            exotic. Say *minority*—

a coiled, dark curl
    a finger might wrap
        itself in. The long
            staircase, and I was

the momentum
    of metal springs
        descending down
            and down,
                a tension

—the long staircase,
    and I was a stacked series
        of spheres finger-tipped
            again into motion,

taut, like a child
    who must please
        the elders and doesn't
            know how, a curl pulled

thin. I wanted to be
    a reckoning, to tornado
        into each day's hard
            hands, that wanton

lurching forward
      in the dark, another
            soaked black ringlet,
                   that sudden halting—

WHAT THIS ELEGY WANTS

It doesn't want a handful of puffed rice
tossed with mustard oil and chopped chilies,

but wants to understand why a firefly
flares off then on, wants another throatful

or three of whiskey. This elegy is trying
hard to understand how we all become

corpses, but I'm trying to understand
permanence, because this elegy wants

to be the streetlamp above me that darkens
as sudden as a child who, in death, remains

a child. Somewhere, there is a man meant
for me, or maybe just to fall asleep beside me.

Across two oceans, there is a world where
I thought I could live without grief. There,

I watched a vendor reach with hands of lace
towards a woman who looked like me. There,

I fingered bolts of satin I never meant to buy.
There, no one said her name. How to look

into the abyss without leaning forward? How
to gather the morning's flustered shadows

into a river? Tonight, I will watch a man I could
love walk past, hefting another woman's child.

He doesn't look at me. I won't wonder if I
wanted him to. This elegy wonders why

it's so hard to say, *I always miss you. Wait,*
she might have said. *But didn't you want*

your palms to be coated in mustard oil? Did you
really want to forget the damp scent of my grave?

TO THE BANGLADESHI CAB DRIVER IN SAN FRANCISCO

Half-drunk, I don't do more than lean
my head against the back of your seat,
straining to hear. You call your brother

to wake him from slumber. We drive up
hills past palm trees and sidewalks chalked
yellow, your voice soft as you murmur

in the language fed to me from birth.
I strain to hear each known word:
bhai=brother, bon=sister, bhaat=rice,

daal=lentils. After the nightly fares, do you
replace slacks for a lunghi, shoes for chappals?
Do you close your fingers into the sharp beak

of a hungry crow to gather the last bits
of bhaat and daal? I could open my mouth to you
in the register I know we know, but don't,

or won't. I can't go back to summers spent unfurling
in heat beside vendors uncapping bottles of Fanta, just
to weave hours striped with palm trees into jute-joyous

shacks. Bhai, here it is spring. Drive past
these parks of dew-carcassed grass, the smooth
and bright limbs heaped carelessly. Drive

ocean-ward. Park at the dock, where used
condoms remain half-submerged in sand.
Cyan water will forgive bottles bullied

into shards, such glittering emerald ghosts
of revelry or remorse. Swim homeward. There,
it's noon: time enough for the sun to coax out

the perfume of a shapla lily's pink petals,
kissed by the lips of a garment worker
whose ankle sings with bells as she pedals.

TO THE LITTLEST BROTHER

hey chotto-bhai, heard
          they promoted you to first commander
of the old crew. heard

←

          you can turn the knots back into ropes
now, that they're with
          you. as for me, i'm still fighting not to be

←

a djinn or hate-burnt spire.
          i haven't razored my wrists, tho,
or pilfered the pills to end

←

          the endless clang and clamor of oilchange-
whatshouldweeat-cash-
          register (*ka-ching! ka-ching!* my girl j and i

←

would high-five and say
          any time we saw boys we decided to confuse
into men). before you

←

          judge, consider: before body there is nobody,
and we all begin
          as small shores. ay, littlest-brother, heard you

←

tie ties by yourself
        now, that out there, there's the right one
to love, that you don't

←

        shake at the table as much anymore. is pink
still your favorite color?
        do you eavesdrop with four ears and two

←

knocked knees?
        listen, the ache of a sister for a brother
isn't obvious or

←

        absent. i swear, not all of us die at war
or in accidents.
        chotto-bhai, the books i left are secrets,

←

underlined beside
        a summer-heavy pecan tree. write past all
the censors. i'll
        grab cheese-sticks, high-five you after,

←

tomorrow. remember?

SOLILOQUIES FROM THE VILLAGE OF ORPHANS AND WIDOWS

During the Liberation War of Bangladesh in 1971, collaborators led the Pakistani army to Sohagpur village. In one day, they killed 164 men. Fifty-seven women survived the atrocities, only to live out life as widows. Sohagpur (Village of Love) was renamed Bidhoba Palli (Village of Widows).

The army killed every male in the village, every male.
When the army was gone, there was not a single man left to bury the dead.
We had to drag the bodies ourselves and bury them.
—anonymous

Sharmila, why do you go on,
I thought but did not ask,
about the thatched hut
where, yes, as you've said,
you had your first, second
third, fourth, fifth child?
But I kept grinding
the rice into flour I loved
        to make fragrant
with water from dawn's
pond. He'd pull
my hair ("Chup koro, Sharmila!"
I yelled). Later, I sidled over
to lay upon her soft arm.
"Maaf koro," I cried.
He had hurt me. Yes,
I did miss him—

but what reason was that
to not apologize?

We married
at the cemetery.
My brother held the bouquet:
one black rose
and seven white marigolds.
I was a pinch of red clay.
A bright and transparent
feeling did not graft. The groom
stood beside me. I did not
think of what I was promising:
companion
corpse. I ached
for the chokecherry tree
in the old village.
Maa would grind anise seed
into gold dust.
Baba mended
wide fish nets
on days
fat with sky
and sun-crushed fallow . . .
Do you swear to obey?
I smirked.

My brother cut
the ribbon
cuffing my hand
to his. *Run,*
he bellowed. Below, the dead
continue their silent
and patient work.
Yes, Sharmila. It is my turn to cook.

I know
his hand
is not pressed
anymore against

my breastplate
trying to pull me open
when I curl into
a swan.

You'll thank me
later, he'd smile.
Are you awake,
lazy? calls Nahar
from the fresh-
rained pond.

"Ji, Ji!" I trill,

lifting my beak
from the steel feathers
still

sprouting along
my spine.

But that was back
when Nahar's boy
    would sit so content just okaane
          on his blue-painted stool.
We'd peel onions,
his favorites, the small

purple ones—he loved to read
those smarty-tarty books, share with us old aunties the good bits
from lives
    stranger than ours!
But that was before . . .
before.

    I can't bear to look

when twilight invites back all the smriti of yesteryear—
her eyes turn without her—back to

his slate—his name

    in chalk none of us
        dare erase.

I was told I should say
no and taught to say
yes—so,
everyday,
it's *okay*
that jumps out of my throat,
ponds full of them, so many lazy
ferengi frogs . . . *okay, okay,* aachcha, *okay, okay,*
tikh hai, *sure, sure, okay, okay,* we say.
Why don't we hop away
or stop being gross green bloats? Jaah!
I'd rather be a shapla phul: fat, pink, afloat.

Each day began
with the search
for the perfect one.
I was the shadow
his own shadow
made dusking
water as he bent
to blade the reed.
I was the hunger
more terrible than
hunger. He saw
threat
in the yaw
of my harpooning hips.
What you need, he wept,
is purity. I was not
the taint he swore
he'd flay away;
I was the plant
he stripped
into a whip.
He was patient
with his fists.
But the gods gave
him no peace. I
did not weep.
They knew I
was not weak.
I test the knife.
It glints. It
winks.

I squat in the dirt to take a piss
until the promise of rain
makes me sway before washing
        between my thighs,
                        still black as moon-sanded tides
        of Cox's Bazar's shoreline.
                I left every life I knew
                        the night he untied me,
        and, well, the moon fell into my well!
                        I want to share spicy
                chaat with a man
before and after the storm.
                        I want him to marvel at newspaper twirled
                        into a cone. I want him
                to promise me a pendulum
                        of aparajita blossoms to cinch
into an embrace, oh, my ungrasped waist . . . oh
                        well! I will twist myself
                        into a new frenzy of pink chiffon!
                        It is holy
                        to touch ourselves
                        without the permission of the gods!
                I hold my breath
        and teacup.
O Durga Maa!
Send this thirst away
in a fleet of rickshaws!

When I say love,
I mean
each artery of this ink.
When I say quick
conjecture of paper
and potential,
I mean
my desire to designate
your vena cava in charcoal.
When I say, "Ekaane aasho,"
I mean come
before I say *no*,
I mean my quill
tickling your ventricle.
Aaina, my nib
between your teeth.
Name me moth-
fling, lightning-
shudder, milk-
tongue—yes, wolf-
whistle me
into moon-
thorn, unlatch
my orphan window, unpainted
atrium only
sinners dare
enter.

Our pet bunny
Chaandu was thistle white,
moonberry black. When he died,
ahaare, the tornadoes my sister
ugly-cried: the last loss.
I did not.
I wiped clean
a metal box.
I folded
Baba's
sarong
wrong.
I buried
him alone.
It was too
hot to wait.
I went on
until it was done.
Well, Time? I said, finally. Ami
ekaane. *What are you, anyway? Trap, or tree?*
But there was no one
but me at the gateway.

YOUR OWN PALM

O, my daughter, once I was a poor boy
folding peppers into my sarong
to walk three miles to sell, but what
can you tell me of sorrow,
or of the courage it takes to buy
a clock instead of a palmful
of rice to go with the goat
we can't afford to slaughter?
Look at the lines Allah etched
on your own palm: you have
a big brain and a good heart,
still, you don't use either enough!
Once, I walked through a war
beside my brother parallel
to a gray river. Why do you care
about the few damp bills
I didn't give to our mother?
Or the clock I bought to take apart? Well,
I left that country with a palmful
of seeds I've thrown across
this dry, hard Texas. Allah
has blessed me with this vine
that coils upward. I care
so little for what others say, ask
your mother. That nose ring
doesn't suit you, by the way.
Once, you were small enough
to cradle. There was a coil
in that clock made of metal . . . O,
that something so small can matter . . .
                    No, daughter, I
don't need a glass of water. Look,

this will grow into maatir neeche aloo.
In the spring, you see, its purple leaves
will be the size of your own palm.
In the village, there is a saying:
"Dhuniya dhari, kochu pathar paani."
I don't know where the clock is
or how much it's worth! There was
not enough for kerosene . . . why
do you always ask what can't be answered?

CONSIDER THE HANDS ONCE SMALLER

It is like this. The night is lonely
until it isn't. You bite your tongue
after eating orange rubbed with chili
before wishing for a kiss
from the man whose questions
unearth the softness in you.
We share with each other the names
of our dying. We buy oranges in cities

gnawing then burying the cadavers
of their own opulent dreams.
We tell each other to dream.
When you send me pictures
you're collecting of women
in your family smiling, I unhinge.
It is like this. The night is our hair
inking the torsos of men into reliquaries.

I don't know why we don't know our own holiness,
but once you were a little girl, and so was I.

DARK PAIRING

I am learning to love you,

        my fingers unruly.

What thrives without
                special treatment?

Not all species are hardy,
    easy to grow from seed. Let us

remember how innocent we were.

Some species
                prefer full sun, others tolerate
the shade—
dude, didn't I know you first

by your body's particulate sweat?—Some

species are overlooked, mistaken
            for weeds, choked by the neighboring,

and there was a time I was one
      of many thin stalks none would want to cut.

You move among the many-
        breasted hives, my heart under your foot,

sister of a stone. It's true I gave

you the memory of my sorrow to keep, seed
        of her ghost—

and you, here like this,
                         pressing back—it comes

        back readily, and I turn

to you, caught,
         our mouths opening. I misjudged

my father most, it was my own

                hard darkening—toughest of all species,

I survive on my own, and though the propensity to hybridize creates confusion,

                                you and I continue to bend into and away

from each other, dark pairing. I understand

now the fear
of a child growing
                         into a woman, one

        who might show love—kneeling down

        to drink again the riotous tangling of my legs in yours.

                        Do we have to cut away rungs from this
wild climbing? Here

is such verdant and frost-
                burnt propagating.
                                Is it grace?

POETRY RECITATION AT
ST. CATHERINE'S SCHOOL FOR GIRLS

> If this were the beginning of a poem, he would have called the thing he felt
> inside him the silence of snow.   —Orhan Pamuk

Before the hanging cross, the girls
take turns standing at attention before
us with eyes closed or hands clasped,

headbands bright green or bangles
yellow, glints that fill the silence like
falling snow. They recite poems they

have carried in their mouths for days,
and my desire to go back, to be one
among these slender, long-haired girls

is a thistle, sharp and twisting at my
side. The words *psalm*, *blessing*, *lord*,
rise in me like bees heavy with pollen,

and the teenager I once was unzips
herself from me, shows up, a crocus
bristling through snow. She's back

in the old chapel where the priest
again lifts into the air the Bible,
declaims about the kingdom of God,

gifts promised only the righteous—
the girl I was, heavy and slow in her
thick glasses, knew she would never

enter heaven, never be these pretty girls
singing, arms pale and slim as the white
birch whose branches, dappled with gold,

shade the stained glass window. In Pamuk's
novel, *Snow*, the headscarf girls in eastern Turkey
hang themselves rather than go uncovered,

and I still want that certainty of conviction,
even as the self beside me pulls on her hair,
sucks long strands of it deep into her mouth—

so I gather her in my arms, shake her, tell
her to listen, that the sky will always happen,
these branches. *Sometimes, it causes me*

to tremble, tremble, she sings beside these
girls who will grow into or away from their own
bodies, and I know I must push the heavy

amber of her back inside me. Help me, Lord.
There are so many bodies inside this one.

SEX OR SLEEP OR SILK

You are the night
that is sometimes
a highway, fields
blurred by speed
in which wild lives
don't stop glowering.
What is meant by
the word recovery?
Aftermath is red dirt,
red dirt, red dirt and you
are creases of crickets
thicketing corners
of this and every room
I decide that I am
safe. You are still
below ground,
an infinite autumn.
I am the flaunting
of this flesh that eats,
fucks, bathes, waits—
I'm done cataloguing
loss. I'll sand glossy
the corners of rib-
cages that I empty,
that empty me. I will
spur my skin into sex
or sleep or silk.
Your dresses still
hang in a closet
unworn and untouched.
So what if I am

phantom-bruise, torn
tether, feral orphan?
I'm telling you now, I
am never going to die.

GREAT MATERIAL

There were the blue-tied garbage bags
bulging with her dresses. Then, the buzz
of junebugs on nights I sat on the roof alone
and asked where my sister was until I felt stupid

and stopped. What do you say to the dead?
How can we rejoin them when we fall apart
in the safety net below? Does she know
her friends Lauren and Cameron played

house after she died, set a place for her
at a play dinner table? As though she
might stop by for a few bites of air
from empty plates with spoons empty

of her short seven years on this planet . . .
it unbottles me, how precisely they lamented
her. *What great material*, the conference
well-wisher said. *Can't wait to read that poem.*

Here it is then, now. The crinkle of your laughter.
The beetles pouring into your eyes as we toast you.

YOU ASK WHY WRITE ABOUT IT AGAIN

A child's handprints are smudged
on cream and green walls, the deaf cannot
                    know the sounds
of their own grief, sleep comes
or does not come.
                    The hand
pressed hard against the pillow
                    does not want
to be the hand that lifts the pen again
to write the word sister, the word silence—
the hand desires
                    blossoms, instead:
bluebonnets, soft whorls of wax, pooled.
The blade held by
                    the hand is a blade
even when used for crushing
and not cutting: dill, cardamom, a bulb
of garlic, pink and yellow pills.
                    We want to be pen
and blade and window, are stains on walls
instead—praise the lanterns mottled
with the heft and shimmer of sorrow
                    unnamed but questioned,
praise sun-red tumbleweeds
and black candle, the metal canisters brimming
with lentils, cumin,
                    failure. Praise
the ailanthus moth spinning
                    its coarse silk—
it cannot stop, it must not.

THE HIDDEN REGISTER OF SOLACE

(First waking)

to learn that each of your fingers
can be swallowed by mist
but remain intact, and that

you can always flex the calves
allowing you to pedal
far from

(first happiness)

the receding figures of everyone
the summer you learned
to ride that old blue bike before

(first pulse)

the silken emancipation
of a handkerchief
from the mystery of your grandfather's

pocket, the handful
of invisible everything—
you tell your love it is okay to feel

(first mercy)

petals of musk mallow sedating
the wind into momentary
slowness

(first love)

and first, love,
the moment you caught
a glimpse of yourself standing

in the long unending plane
of a tinted window—
then skin, skin, skin,

torso, teeth, wrist,
the birds of hair, pierced to heart

(first beginnings)

cannot be distinguished by the eye—

SELF-PORTRAIT AS ARTEMIS

It wasn't long before I rose
into the silk of my night-robes

and swilled the stars
and the beetles

back into sweetness—even my fingernails
carry my likeness, and I smudge

the marrow of myself
into light. I whisper street-

car, ardor, midnight
into the ears of the soldier

so he will forget everything
but the eyes of the night nurse

whose hair shines beneath
the prow of her white cap.

In the end, it is me
he shipwrecks. O arrow.

My arms knot as I pluck
the lone string tauter.

O crossbow. I kneel. He oozes,
and the grasses and red wasp

knock him back from my sight.
The night braids my hair.

I do not dream. I glow.

THE DISTANCE BETWEEN FIRE AND STONE

I've never told the truth
about anything: not that

I've often found the defiance
of forest fires more stunning

than the pre-planned blooms
of fireworks, not the night I caught

my friend cutting her mom's pills
in half in the dark. I've tried

to accept that the lesson learned
from a plane barreling into a pentagon

is that fire will always only ever
come close to ravishing stone,

but the truth is, I still don't entirely
understand the expanse between

stacks of planks of acres of trees
and the stacks of paper they become,

small bits of which Fermi let drift
from his fingers during the detonation

of the first atomic bomb. The truth is,
across each narrow road two oceans

from here, men speak to each other
most honestly with their car horns.

THE ERROR OF ECHO

The day I won the school spelling bee,
Jeff Wood was in 8th grade,
and I was in 4th. I think of him
at odd times, like standing in front
of a tea kettle, and even now I feel bad
his friends teased him the rest of the day
for losing by misspelling the word
echo.

        As in, reflection of sound,
        the wistful whispering of salaat
        in every corner of the mosque.
        As in, those blue-dark almost-mornings.

Do you hear an echo? they taunted
when he tried to speak—*E-C-O*,
Jeff had sounded out cool and slow,
hands easy in the pockets
of his Wranglers. (That football-shaped
belt buckle, the cafeteria where I spent
hours wishing I was someone, anyone else).
E-C-O.

        As in, prefix for ecosystem,
        as in, I am alive, a small part
        of some bewildered and bewitching
        series of frameworks.

After, I was embarrassed, the way
you are when you're young
and don't know how to hold
the possibility of your own potential.
Mrs. Simmons handed me
a trophy, and Jeff and I must've

shaken hands. Do you hear an
echo?

As in, nymph of rock and ravine cursed
to endlessly repeat the voice of another.
As in, I can't help but speak
for fear the voice I'll hear is my own.

THE DOORS TO TRINITY

I never lost 'em. Here they are,
      scratch-handled, gum-gunked.
           I didn't learn to reach higher,

I just did, first on my toddling toes.
      I did learn to borrow: rides from strangers,
           how to dress or laugh, cash stacked

in aluminum foil meant for villagers
      too far away for me to care.
           Yeah, I did that. Snuck off

to unwrap my own morals:
      for a card to call a boy in another
           state who didn't want me, rings

that gave my knuckles grass-colored scars,
      and a diary to carry my aches in.
           I lied and stole and swallowed.

I didn't notice all the lesions
      I hadn't meant to hoard.
           I wouldn't be held or told.

Yesterday was tomorrow.
      I was gentler then, not yet hollowed.
           But always unkempt, even if authored.

First, the tornadoed cubbyhole damp
      with forged permission slips, then
           the locker packed with pens I chewed

into twizzled plastic fodder, or wallpapered
        with magazine cutouts of boys grinning
                in different colors. Then, I began to rub out

the foulest parts of me until I was vellum.
        I stayed smudged anyway, a blue pat
                of drugstore eye-shadow brush-softened.

You know how it all stretches
        and slows? One minute you're falling
                on your diapered ass for the first time

and then the next mistake keeps you thirsting
        for more—I became crucifix and spear,
                cut and colored glass, the hymns

I didn't not sing at home.
        Even now I can't help
                but stick out all my tongues.

I am chosen, I prayed, I was born.
        I took a right, a left, and another left.
                I'm sometimes late, but I do love

to run a palm all alone around
        the shining altar. I still believe
                I could be, like y'all said, anything

I wanted. When I did, the light
        never seemed to falter. I know y'all
                saw me sit with my feet up

in those high thrones I called fancy
        chairs. How fat with love,
                my wild, orange-scented hair.

DIARY

She came into my room again
smelling of gardenias to thumb
through the private pages
tucked below my pillow.
Some days, helplessness
is a humidity that balms
the windows of any room.
You and I fucked, and now I listen
again to this creased crackle
of paper I keep purpling
with the roll call of my aches
and their sorrows. You suckled
from my throat the petals
of her perfume's glass bottle
I drank from to quench
my anger's thirst. I still call to her
with a mouthful of pollen.
Watch her turn to me.

There are questions
we refuse to ask or answer.

My shadow bloomed
behind hers, across
you. We danced like that,
a hand around my throat,
a hand around yours.

APOLOGY FROM A MUSLIM ORPHAN

I know you know
how to shame into obedience
the long chain tethering lawnmower
to fence. And in your garden
are no chrysanthemums, no hem
of lace from the headscarf
I loose for him at my choosing.
Around my throat still twines a thin line
from when, in another life, I was
guillotined. I know you know
how to slap a child across the face
with a sandal.
Forgive me. I love when he tells me to be
the water you siphon into the roots
of your trees. In that life,
I was your enemy and silverleaf.
In this one, the child you struck was me.

SEARCHLIGHT PAYAR

You fell for them, again they flew, your mouth-split lies. Devils!
Why do they breed, what do they need? Hate-hot hammers? Anvils?

Gore-blunt scissors? Wrists in sharp fists? Breasts in red teeth? Don't, please—
we're galaxies, wet tulip trees, not enemies, blood fees.

Who did I hurt, a threat to what, what blaze to snuff? Power.
You gave me up, you gave us up, you gave you up. Coward.

AUBADE WITH SAGE AND LEMON

First I said, yes, here
by the light. The dark
has its own blindfold,
the pearls of the eyes
of anyone who will leave
you—sprig of sage

for your hair, he said.
Rind of lemon for
your fingers, and la
ilaha illallah I whistled,
though the dawn eats
its own faith, rubs aromatics

into the question of what
comes after the next air raid
or bombing or shooting
and the morning is blank
and the sun shines down
on another blatant river

of limbs. First I said,
tomorrow, then, now,
I'll leave now, while
it's still safe. A few
more minutes, love,
he said, a few more

hours. Just trust,
he said. I said inshallah
to the sprig of sage
and the rind of lemon

until the uniformed man
smiled and raised his gun

higher towards the sound
a human body makes
when it's about to fly.
I made no sound
but the sound a wraith
makes as it sings

itself goodbye.
I said sprig, said rind—
and watched him die.
First I begged, grave.
Then I said, above, and lifted
the pen in my wing even higher.

BECAUSE THERE'S STILL A SKY, JUNEBUG

I turn on the porchlight
so the insects *will* come,
so my skin that drank of you
can marvel at how
quickly it becomes enraged,
a luscious feast. I'm waiting
to hear myself crystallize
with revelation.
Who stands guard at rooms locked into tombs?
Who will dictate the order
in which we're consumed?
—I turn the light off,
but who taught me to stay quiet
when the power is down?
You're so sweet, men say to me,
but tonight, I want
no one. Tonight, a drone
in Yemen detonates and rends the sky,
and in my father's garden,
drone is a stingless bee unable
to make honey.
I crush the antennae, regard
the exoskeleton. Do we ever learn
that we're given weapons
to be vicious so we can be sweet?
I look up,
because there is still a sky, the junebug
that whirs across it, because
there is still a head-scarfed girl
who sucks the sugar
from a ginger candy
before she explodes—I look up,
and the sky still flints with so many stars. Above me.
Above you.

I TOLD THE WATER

for Flint, Michigan

I told the water   You're right

    the poor are
        broken sidewalks

we try to avoid

Told it   the map of you   folds   into corners

    small enough   to swallow   I told the water

You only exist because of thirst

    But beside your sour membrane   we lie

        facedown in dirt

The first time   my father threw me into you

    I became hieroglyph   a wet braid

        caught   in your throat

I knew then   how *war* was possible

            the urge

to defy gravity   to dis-
        arm another

    I knew then we'd kill

to be your mirror   You   black-eyed barnacle

You   graveyard

of windows   I told the water

Last night I walked out onto the ice

wearing only my skin

You couldn't tell me   not to

MOTHER

I woke alone. I had been dreaming of cat-sized blood ants in my blood's homeland, of women who undrape wet and green fields from their torsos. Mother, it was cold. What used to be my arm ached. Nails were hammered to cohere my splintered shoulder. Cotton was pushed between my legs to staunch that month's moon. It was some time before I remembered that light can't be brushed on to anyone else's shoulders, and I couldn't stop wondering why the ocean inside the drunkard never sleeps. I left the blankness of those walls, and hobbled to where the world was free. I woke alone. Mother, I sat below a tree. It was asleep in a child while cannons fired across fields of cotton. The child knew how to cut and sand the tree into planks and hammer them across her windows. It had been a long time since she'd seen the ocean. She was used to drinking smoke. *Each time a branch grows back*, she mourned, *I shake*. I asked if she knew where my mother was. The child put her hand on my shoulder. She touched her saw to where I was most free. You woke, and held out your arms to me. Mother: the napping tree in the village inside of me. You folded me back into fifths, lay me in my sweet acorn cradle. You wrapped my favorite blanket, a black leaf, around me.

VARIATIONS ON A CEMETERY IN SUMMER

—July 4, 2014

An ant travels across
time and up my leg and I let
her. If bitten, I'll dream
tonight of the songs
they sing to busy themselves
with antennaed industries.

*

Say of the bees that they offer us
more sugar than sting—

*

The dead love the scent
of flowers in summer, the soft
fog of their last lives embraces
the waists of trees, infinite
spiral of infinite fabric.

*

I've loved the mouth-
punctured leaves best always.
Tonight I'll rock back and forth
on my porch beside death,
stitch lapfuls with her
into a sun-blessed lace dress.

*

This world: at war with its own whirl—

*

I press my tongue to moss,
to kiss until I too grow
branches too strong to be jostled.

*

Before I knew time I used to dream
unspun beneath the sun until
I was weightless, until neither
thigh nor sleep
anchored me to the ground.

*

A flag crinkles the breeze
with its histories.
A country sighs, struggles
to remember to gaze
at its own stories of stars.

*

My god, these barely malleable rhymes—

*

When lying down among
the breathing, dream of skies
vaster than ours. When lying
beside the dead, dream
clean the dandelions of your scars.

. . . BUT YOU CAN'T STAY HERE

Everyday, I rack up some new cost I can't repay,
and even now, I'm reluctant to run to the door
on nights the world sizzles with drizzle-drama,

all that drop and give me more. Tonight, the ghouls
are later than usual. *Isn't it polite to wait before*
serving the first course? I murmur to my forebears

as they slide the biryani from the oven.
Uncover the lime wedges and old resentments,
they reply, so I do. At last, we lick each virtue

from our plates with satisfaction, then settle in
to savor spoonfuls of milk-softened toast
without dreading tomorrow morning's inevitable

convo about self-worth. Speaking of, today
I stepped on the cat's tail and sprang back
in apology, but when she didn't yelp and dash,

I remembered: there was no tail, there was no cat.

FABLE OF THE FIRSTBORN

In the beginning, I was neither image
nor identity. Time was a quickening;
I was my own dark-watered well.
There was no hankering there, just
another native world and its wishes.
Who is Memory? Why does she matter
to History? Their far-off laughter uncurled
me—I stretched out to hear more closely.

In the beginning, I was born a man-girl
with teeth for toes and a headful
of hair hiding the nubs of horns.
This was before ally or self-portrait,
prodigal performer or forgotten prop. Soon,
I was collecting sounds I mimicked
at my elders' commands to avoid my own
noise. I found myself hiding in a closet

beside bags of clothes only the dead would wear.
That wasn't the first time I spooned myself.
Yes, there were large and small storms.
I had a sister until the accident, and a brother
was willed after months of grief-graft.
By then, I was already distant, a tumbleweed
rubbing my thorns late into the night
when those yesteryears sidle near.

Isn't that why you're here? In the end,
there's only one way to begin
an origin story: at the beginning. I know
a good one: a monster named Joy-

in-the-Margins learns the nature of light
by revising the dark into song with every
register of her seven tongues.
Ready? Let's begin. Verse 0. Surah 1.

I do not fear time.
Nina Simone

NOTES

The epigraph in "Register of Eliminated Villages" wouldn't exist without an episode of *Frontline*, in 2002, with Kanan Makiya: "I have a register which lists 397 eliminated villages, Kurdish villages in northern Iraq. . . . The work is called 'The Register of Eliminated Villages.' You flip the pages, beautifully scripted and done with a pencil. Then the writer of this book has covered it, folded it very neatly with a nice, great big book cover made of paper, with great big white flowers against a red background. It's a very decorative, pretty thing. . . . You look at this person who has taken such immaculate care of this book, which records the destruction of 397 Kurdish villages. . . . You look at the book and you know you're touching evil somehow."

"The Hidden Register of Hunger" wouldn't exist without Olena Kalytiak Davis and James Merrill.

"Djinn in Need of a Bitch" wouldn't exist without Lynda Hull.

"Before the Accident, and After" wouldn't exist without Jenny Boychuk and Laura Kasischke.

"100 Bells" wouldn't exist without Vievee Francis and her poem "Say It, Say It Anyway You Can" from *Horse in the Dark*.

The italicized lines in "The Hidden Register of Submission" are from Pauline Réage's *Story of O* (originally published in 1954).

"Self-Portrait as Slinky" wouldn't exist without the Kenyon Review Writers Workshop and Jake Adam York.

"What This Elegy Wants" wouldn't exist without Jon Pineda.

"To the Littlest Brother" wouldn't exist without Tausif Faizullah and Jaundréa "Javon" Clay.

"Your Own Palm" wouldn't exist without AM Faiz.

"Consider the Hands Once Smaller" wouldn't exist without Durba Mitra.

"Dark Pairing" wouldn't exist without lines from Sylvia Plath's "The Beekeeper's Daughter" from *Ariel*.

"Poetry Recitation at St. Catherine's School for Girls" wouldn't exist without its epigraph, from Orhan Pamuk's *Snow*, as well as lines from "Were You There," first published in William Eleazar Barton's *Old Plantation Hymns* (1899).

"The Hidden Register of Solace" wouldn't exist without Lucretius.

"The Error of Echo" wouldn't exist without Jeff Wood.

"Diary" wouldn't exist without Jehanne Dubrow.

"Apology from a Muslim Orphan" wouldn't exist without Czeslaw Milosz, Robert Lowell, and the Kenyon Review Young Writers Workshop.

"Variations on a Cemetery in Summer" wouldn't exist without Wallace Stevens and the Kenyon Review Young Writers Workshop.

The closing and opening epigraphs are from Nina Simone's live cover of lyricist Sandy Denny's "Who Knows Where the Time Goes," originally recorded October 26, 1969, in New York, Philharmonic Hall, for her album *Black Gold* (1970).

ACKNOWLEDGMENTS

Thank you to the following periodicals and anthologies in which earlier versions of these poems first appeared:

The Academy of American Poets Poem-a-Day, "Self-Portrait as Artemis," "Apology from a Muslim Orphan," "Your Own Palm"

The American Poetry Review, "West Texas Nocturne"

Best New Poets 2013: 50 Poems from Emerging Writers, "Self-Portrait as Slinky"

Blackbird, "Djinn in Need of a Bitch" as "Ramadan Nocturne"

B O D Y Literature, "Your Own Country"

The Book of Scented Things: 100 Contemporary Poems about Perfume, "Diary"

BuzzFeed, "Aubade with Sage and Lemon"

Copper Nickel, "You Ask Why Write about It Again"

diode, "Acolyte"

Hobart, "The Hidden Register of Hunger," "The Hidden Register of Submission," "Consider the Hands Once Smaller"

The Journal, "Sex or Sleep or Silk," "The Distance between Fire and Stone"

jubilat, "Mother"

The Kenyon Review, "The Hidden Register of Solace"

Michigan Quarterly Review, "I Told the Water," "Variations on a Cemetery in Summer"

The Missouri Review, "To the Bangladeshi Cab Driver in San Francisco," "Poetry Recitation at St. Catherine's School for Girls"

Muzzle Magazine, "Dark Pairing"

The Nation, "Fable of the Firstborn"

New England Review, "What This Elegy Wants" as "The Streetlamp above Me Darkens"

The New Republic, "Before the Accident, and After"

Ninth Letter, "Self-Portrait as Slinky"

Oxford American, "Because There's Still a Sky, Junebug"

Passages North, "Register of Eliminated Villages"

Ploughshares, "Self-Portrait as Mango"

Poet Lore, "The Error of Echo"

Poetry, "100 Bells"

Pushcart Prize XXXIX: Best of the Small Presses 2015 Edition, "What This Elegy
   Wants" as "The Streetlamp above Me Darkens"

Pushcart Prize XLI: Best of the Small Presses 2017 Edition, "100 Bells"

Pushcart Prize XLII: Best of the Small Presses 2018 Edition, "I Told the Water"

South Dakota Review, "The Performance of No One's Fingers" as "Prodigy," "IV
   and Make-Up Homework"

Tin House (online), "Soliloquies from the Village of Orphans and Widows"

This book wouldn't exist without the support of friends, colleagues, mentors, professors, editors, workshop participants, organizations, institutions, and family members. Many thanks to each of you, especially my parents for their many gifts, including the Slinky, the women of Sohagpur for their strength and stories, the Kenyon Review Young Writers Workshop for always reminding me, the University of Michigan Helen Zell Writers' Program for the fellowship of time, space, and the best crew, Dinah Barry for the mothering, Big Sean for the artist motivation ("Aw damn, I'm illuminated!"), Tommye Blount for Saturdays or Sundays, Jenny Boychuk for the last poem prompt, Jaundréa "Javon" Clay for the telepathic ka-ching, Monica Chowdhury for transatlantic big-sistering, Lawrence Minh-Bui Davis for believing, Tausif Faizullah for asking me to text him a poem, francine j. harris for music and musings, Anna Claire Hodge for dreaming, Laura Kasischke for her mentorship, Cynthia Grier Lotze for bread and bedtime, Pete Mathes for the playlisting, Airea D. Matthews for the camaraderie, Jamaal May for comradeship in craft and crime, Rachel McKibbens for the raging, Monica Patel for the hidden gifts, Jeff Shotts for patiently reading and rereading, Maya West for the sanity, and everyone for the future memories.

TARFIA FAIZULLAH was born in 1980 in Brooklyn, New York, and raised in Midland, Texas. She is the author of a previous poetry collection, *Seam*, winner of a VIDA Award, a GLCA New Writers' Award, a Milton Kessler First Book Award, Drake University Emerging Writer Award, and other honors. Her poems are published widely in periodicals and anthologies both in the United States and abroad, are translated into Persian, Chinese, Bengali, Tamil, and Spanish, have been featured at the Smithsonian, the Rubin Museum of Art, and elsewhere, and are the recipients of multiple awards, including three Pushcart Prizes, the Frederick Bock Prize from *Poetry*, and others. In 2016, she was recognized by Harvard Law School's Women Inspiring Change. Faizullah currently teaches in the University of Michigan Helen Zell Writers' Program as the Nicholas Delbanco Visiting Professor in Poetry. She believes in destiny.

The text of *Registers of Illuminated Villages* is set in Minion Pro.
Book design by Rachel Holscher.
Composition by Bookmobile Design & Digital Publisher Services,
Minneapolis, Minnesota.
Manufactured by Versa Press on acid-free,
30 percent postconsumer wastepaper.

THE HIDDEN REGISTER OF ASTONISHMENT

You always were your own astonished twin, your own

shell garden. (Don't remark on the past, that old archer).

Ask when! the crickets whir. Ask, then, before you drown

in the blasphemy of glass crushed by kin. Discover

shark's eye, saw-tooth, hermit turtle, arrow, wentletrap,

a tidal wave inside your shin, the itch of sin and tin.

He pressed his teeth to you; you knew; you grew vast.

What does it mean to give in? More time for revision.

Heave your last doubts into the helixes of tomorrow.

The sound of crickets is a fringed shawl, you swear.

Astonish yourself; unattach in front of his mirror.

You'll press your teeth to him; he'll know your answer.

He's visited your village before. You're almost near

the city. Only you can invite him to your front door.